ISBN 978-1-334-36501-0
PIBN 10571357

This book is a reproduction of an important historical work. Forgotten Books uses
state-of-the-art technology to digitally reconstruct the work, preserving the original format
whilst repairing imperfections present in the aged copy. In rare cases, an imperfection in
the original, such as a blemish or missing page, may be replicated in our edition. We do,
however, repair the vast majority of imperfections successfully; any imperfections that
remain are intentionally left to preserve the state of such historical works.

English
Français
Deutsche
Italiano
Español
Português

www.forgottenbooks.com

Mythology Photography **Fiction**
Fishing Christianity **Art** Cooking
Essays Buddhism Freemasonry
Medicine **Biology** Music **Ancient
Egypt** Evolution Carpentry Physics
Dance Geology **Mathematics** Fitness
Shakespeare **Folklore** Yoga Marketing
Confidence Immortality Biographies
Poetry **Psychology** Witchcraft
Electronics Chemistry History **Law**
Accounting **Philosophy** Anthropology
Alchemy Drama Quantum Mechanics
Atheism Sexual Health **Ancient History**
Entrepreneurship Languages Sport
Paleontology Needlework Islam
Metaphysics Investment Archaeology
Parenting Statistics Criminology
Motivational

[*Reprinted from the Trans. Roy. Soc. of Literature, Vol.* xii, *Part* 1, 1879.]

THE OGHAM-RUNES AND EL-MUSHAJJAR:

A Study.

BY RICHARD F. BURTON, M.R.A.S.

(Read January 22, 1879.)

PART I.

The Ogham-Runes.

In treating this first portion of my subject, the Ogham-Runes, I have made free use of the materials collected by Dr. Charles Graves, Prof. John Rhys, and other students, ending it with my own work in the Orkney Islands.

The Ogham character, the "fair writing" of ancient Irish literature, is called the *Bobel-loth,* *Bethluis* or *Bethluisnion,* from its initial letters, like the Græco-Phœnician "Alphabeta," and the Arabo-Hebrew "Abjad." It may briefly be described as formed by straight or curved strokes, of various lengths, disposed either perpendicularly or obliquely to an angle of the substance upon which the letters were incised, punched, or rubbed. In monuments supposed to be more modern, the letters were traced,

b

not on the edge, but upon the face of the recipient
surface; the latter was originally wood, staves and
tablets; then stone, rude or worked; and, lastly, metal,
silver, and rarely iron.   The place of the bevel was
often taken by a real or an imaginary perpendicular,
or horizontal, bisecting the shortest notches representing vowel-cuts; or, more generally, by a Fleasgh,
stem-line, trunk-line, or Rune-Staff.   According to
the Rev. Charles Graves,[1] "The continuous stem-
line along which the Ogham letters are ranged is
termed the *ridge* (ᚁᚏᚒᚔᚋ) ;   each short   stroke,
perpendicular or oblique to it, is called a *twig*
(ᚠᚂᚓᚐᚌᚏ;   in the plural ᚠᚂᚓᚐᚏᚷᚐ)."   That authority
also opines that the stem-line, as a rule or guide, like
the Devanágari-Hindú, was borrowed from the Runic
" Staf."

The " Tract on Oghams " and Irish grammatical
treatises[2] contain some eighty different modifications of the Ogham alphabet, while Wormius enu-
merates twelve varieties of the Runes proper—most
of them mere freaks of fancy, like similar prelusions
in the East.[3]   The following is the first on the list,
and it is certainly that which derives most directly
from the old Orient home.

---

[1] " Paper on the Ogham Character."   Proceedings of the Royal
Irish Academy, vol. iv, part 2, p. 360.

[2] The " Tract " is in the " Book of Ballymote," written about the ninth
century, and assuming its present form in the fourteenth.   The treatise
is the " Precepta Doctorum " (Uᴘᴀɪcepᴛ or Uᴘᴘɪcheᴢna neɪᴣeaᴘ or n'eɪᴣeᴘ),
the Primer (Precepts) of the Bards, composed in the ninth or tenth
century, and found in the " Book of Lecan," a manuscript dating from
A.D. 1417.   It is "said to have been composed in the first century."
(p. xxviii., John O'Donovan's Irish Grammar, Dublin, 1845.)

[3] See " Ancient Alphabets and Hieroglyphic Characters explained,"
&c., by Joseph Hammer.   London, 1806.

b l ꜰ ꞃ n   h ꝺ ꞇ c   q   m ᵹ   nᵹ ᴊᴄ   ꝑ   a o u e ɪ

The number and the power of the letters are given, as above, by the author of the "Paper on Oghams."[4] I am aware that this form in which the directing-line has been cut up to make steps is held by some scholars to be a "sort of artificial ladder-Ogham." Yet it is an undoubted revival of the most archaic type; and from it the transition is easy to the modification popularly known, the sixteenth figured in the "Tract on Oghams."

Here evidently the only thing needful was to make the stem strokes of the primitive alphabet a continuous "Fleasgh."

Let us now compare the Ogham proper with what may be called "the Ogham-Runes"; the latter being opposed to *Runogham*[5] or Secret Ogham in such phrases as *Runogham na Fian*—of the Fenians or ancient Irish militiamen. The "Ogham-Runes" represent the three groups of letters (ättcr) generally known as the Futhorc, from the initial six.

Runes.

ᚠ ᚢ ᚦ ᚨ ᚱ ᚲ . ᚷ ᚺ ᛁ ᛃ ᛇ . ᛏ ᛒ ᛚ ᛉ ᛟ .

Corresponding Ogham-Runes.

F u th o r k . H n i a s . T b l m y (ö)

---

[4] *Loc. cit.*, p. 358.

[5] O'Brien and O'Reilly (Dictionaries), translated *Run* by "Secret";
Welsh, *Rhin.*

(The letters may evidently be inverted with the twigs pointing upwards.)

The above specimen of the Ogham-Runes is quoted from Joh. G. Liljegren.[6] In " Hermothena "[7] we find the opinion that this " twig-Rune," corresponding with the " Ogham Craobh " (or virgular Ogham),[8] composed of an upright stem and side branches, suggested the " stepped," " ladder " or primitive Ogham; and hence the perfect popular Ogham. This theory has by no means been generally accepted. Yet it well exemplifies the principle upon which the various Abecedaria were constructed—namely, that the symbol for any letter showed in the first instance its particular group amongst the three; and, secondly, the place which it held in that group. Goransson (Bautil, p. 232) figures an ancient monument on which are a few words written in these "Ogham-Runes " with the twigs (Ṝänneſtreᶜken), the remainder being in the common Runes.

Among the " class-Runes " supposed to have been developed from the " Futhorc " there is a vast variety of forms. We need only quote the variety called Hahal-Runes, whose resemblance is most striking to the " Ogham Craobh."

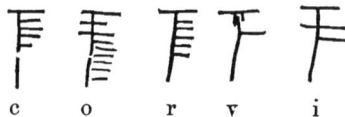

c   o   r   v   i

It is popularly asserted that the inventors, or rather the adapters of the Ogham, gave to its letters the names of trees or plants. So the Chinese

[6] " Runlära," p. 50.

[7] Vol. v., p. 232.

[8] See John O'Donovan's Irish Grammar, Introduction, pp. 34–47— " Craobh Ogham, *i.e., Virgei Characteres* "

" Radical," or key for *Moh*, a tree, is a plain cross $\dagger$ with two additional oblique strokes 木. General Vallancey ("Prospectus of a Dictionary," &c.), who makes this remark, seems to have held that the tree-form was adapted to the name, whereas the virgular shape named the letters. The Arabic El-Mushajjar or El-Shajari, the "branched" or the "tree-like," certainly arose from the appearance of the letters.

In the original Runic Alphabet two letters are called after trees, the thorn and the birch; the latter I have shown[9] is like poplar (*Pippal*), the only term which spread through Europe deriving directly from the old Aryan home (*Bhurja*). To the thorn and the birch the more developed Anglo-Saxon alphabet added four : yew, sedge, oak, and ash. All the Irish letters are made to signify trees or plants ; but at least ten of them are not Irish terms. Amongst foreign words, curious to say, is the second letter of the *Bethluis*, $L = luis =$ a quicken, or mountain ash ; whilst the same is the case with the third letter *n* (*nin*, or *nion*, an ash) in *Bethluisnin* (*Beth-luis-nion?*). The latter term has suggested to some that in old Ogham the letter *n* stood third. But there is nothing in the Uraicept to support this theory. On the contrary, there are passages to show that the word *nin* was " occasionally taken in a general signification, and was used with reference to all the letters of the alphabet in-differently."

All the letters of the Bethluis are called *Feada*,

---

[9] See "Ultima Thule" (Nimmo and Co.) and "Etruscan Bologna."

"woods" or "trees" (Feaδa), a term especially applied to the vowels as being the true "trees." The consonants are *Taobomma* or "side-trees" (ᴛaobomma); and the diphthongs *Forfeada*, "over-trees" or "extra trees." The division of the alphabet is into four *aicme* ("groups") of five letters, each named after its initial. Thus, *b, l, f, s, n* compose the B-group (aicme-b); *h, d, t, c, q* the H-group (aicme-h), and so forth. The five diphthongs (*Forfeada* or "extra trees") *ea, oi, ui, ai* and *ae* become the Foraicme-group (Foɲaɪcme). The words were read from the bottom upwards, often rounding the head of the stone and running down the opposite shoulder. If horizontally disposed, the order was from left to right, like Sanskrit and other Aryans; when written backwards in Semitic fashion, from right to left, secresy was intended.

The groups, both in Runic and in Ogham are : 1. Lines to the left of the Fleasgh when perpendicular, or below it when horizontal ; these are *b, l, f, s, n,* according as they number 1, 2, 3, 4 and 5 characteristic "twigs." 2. Lines to the right or above the line ; *h, d, t, c, q,* (*cu?*). 3. Longer strokes crossing the bevel on the Fleasgh obliquely, *m, n, ng, st* (*z*), *r.* 4. Shorter cuts upon the stem-line usually represent the five vowels, *a, o, u, e, i.* Sometimes

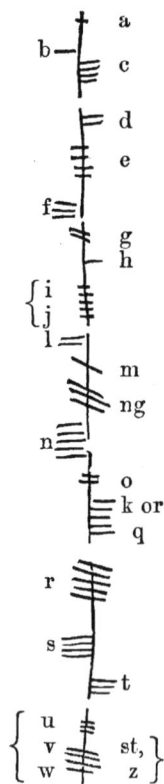

they are mere notches; in other cases they are of considerable length; for instance, in the St. Gall Codex of Priscian, whose eight marginal notes in Ogham are attributed to A.D. 874, 875.

Thus the total characters originally numbered in Runic 16 and in the Ogham 20, or 25, simple and compound. These two illustrations, in which they are compared with the Roman alphabet, show their deficiencies. Of the five diphthongs, only the first (ea) has been found upon the ancient monuments. The next added to it was the second (oi); and lastly came the other three (ui, ia and ea) which were employed occasionally. The absent consonants are j, k (= c, q), p, v, w, x, z. The disappearance of the p, which Bishop Graves[10] holds to be a "primitive letter in the Phœnician alphabet," and which was so much used in Latin, is significant, or rather should be so, to those who hold the Ogham to have been modelled upon the Roman syllabarium. Unknown to the Irish tongue as is the b to Romaic or modern Greek, it is expressed by bh, and the Uraicept assigns as a reason that p is an aspirated b,—which it is not. There are rare and presumedly modern characters for the semi-vowel y, and for the double consonant x (= ks, cs), which was also denoted by cc, ch, ᚦch, and uch. The naso-palatal ng of Sanskrit—a character lost to the abecedaria of Europe—is preserved in Ogham. The z is denoted by ᚏᚈ or ᚏᛓ. Thus Elizabeth and Zacharias become Elistabeth and Stacharias (Liber Hymnorum), and in the Uraicept Greek ζ is written ᚏᚈᛓᚈᚐ (Steta).[11] Finally,

---

[10] Hermothena, iv., 469.

[11] O'Donovan (p. 48) makes z = ts or ds.

several of the signs are supposed to denote different sounds.

I have no intention of entering into the vexed question of Ogham antiquity, or of its pre-Christian versus its post-Christian date. Dr. Graves[12] determines the question as follows : " One of the first things to be remarked in this alphabet is the separation of the letters into consonants and vowels. This arrangement alone ought to have satisfied any scholar that it is the work of a grammarian, and not a genuine primitive alphabet. Again, the vowels are arranged according to the method of the Irish grammarians, who have divided them into two classes, broad and slender. The broad *a, o* (identical in the oldest writings), and *u* are put first; the slender *e* and *i* last." Thus as regards the origin of the Ogham alphabet, the author came to the conclusion that it was introduced into Ireland from Scandinavia or North Germany ; and that it was framed by persons acquainted with the later and developed Runic alphabets, such as those used by the Anglo-Saxons. Dr. O'Connor also doubted the antiquity of the Ogham alphabet. He held that the Irish possessed a primitive abecedarium of 16 letters (like the Runic), all named after trees ; and, consequently, that the tree-shaped letters (*formæ rectilineares*) may be a modern invention.

O'Donovan (1845) makes the *Bobel-loth* alphabet contain 24, and the *Beth-luis-nion* 26 letters. The Reverend Thomas Jones, M.A., reduces the genuine Irish alphabet to 18.

---

[12] *Loc. cit.*, 360.

But these are objections to the alphabet,[13] *not to the characters composing it.* With respect to the artificial distribution of the vowels, Dr. Graves owns in the next sentence that " it was not by any means strictly observed by the earliest writers of this country ;" adding that frequent violations of it are to be found in the "Book of Armagh" and in the monuments of olden time. His argument, founded upon the present systematisation, is absolutely worthless. Ogham. cannot be an original and primitive alphabet in its actual and finished state ; it may have been so in its rude form. A case in point is the modern " Deva-nágari," still used for Prakrit as well as for Sanskrit. That beautiful and philological system is the work of grammarians who knew as much as, and perhaps more than, " Priscian and Donatus." Nothing can be, at any rate nothing is, more artful, more scientific, than its distribution of the sound-symbols. Yet the original and simple abecedarium was old enough, having been simply borrowed from the Phœnicians. We know that the Hindús wrote letters in the days of Alexander, and the Girnár inscriptions prove that the ancient form of the complicated modern alphabet was used in India during the third century B.C. The same may have been the case with the primitive Ogham of 16 or 20 letters. All we can now say is, that either the inscriptions have perished or they are yet to be found ; and no wonder when they were cut on wooden staves, wands, and tablets :

" Barbara fraxineis sculpatur Rhuna tabellis."

(Ammian. Marcell.)

[13] " Critical Essay on the Ancient Inhabitants of the Northern Parts of Britain or Scotland." London, 1729. Chiefly a reply to O'Flaherty's " Ogygia Vindicated."

Bishop Graves himself quotes many remnants of tradition touching the use of Ogham among the heathen Irish—not to speak of the Catholic legend of Fenius Fearsaidh, " great grand-son of Japhet." A story in the " Leabhar na h Uidhri," mentions the Ogham, inscribed on the end of the *Lia* or headstone planted over the grave of King Fothadh Airgthech (the Robber), who ruled Ireland in A.D. 285. The " Book of Ballymote " refers to the Ogham of Fiachrach (ob. A.D. 380). A similar allusion is found in the "Elopement of Deirdré,"[14]—their Ogham names were written.

Again, the Druid Dallan, sent by Eochaidh Airem, King of Ireland, to recover Queen Etaine, " made four wands of yew and wrote in Ogham on them." This event is attributed (Tocmarc Etaine) to B.C. 100. Lastly we are told that in heathen times the Irish " marked everything which was hateful to them in Ogham on the Fé;" the latter being a wand made of the aspen, a " fey " tree, and used for measuring the corpse and its grave. The cave of the New Grange tumulus, ascribed to the Tuath De Danaans, and opened in A.D. 1699, exhibits a few Ogham characters (numerals?) and near them a decided representation of a palm branch.[15] There is another, attributed to pagan ages, on a pillar-stone near Dunloe Castle, county Kerry. We may then hold, with Professor Rhys, that the " origin of Ogham writing is still hidden in darkness."

A note by Bishop Graves on " Scythian letters,"[16]

[14] " Transactions of the Gaelic Society of Dublin," 1808, pp. 127-9.

[15] O'Donovan, *loc. cit.*, pp. 28 and 44. See both figured in Fergusson's "Rude Stone Monuments," p. 207.

[16] " Hermothena," vol. v., p. 252, terminal note.

shows that the "Alans predicted futurity by in-
scribing straight line-sticks with secret enchant-
ments." (Ammian. Marcell. xxxi, § 2, 24.) The
Sortes Prænestinæ of Cicero (De Div. ii, 40) were
"inscribed on oak with marks of ancient letters."
Cæsar (Bell. Gall. ii, c. 53,) speaks of similar *Sortes*
among the Germans ; and Tacitus (Germ. c. x.) notes
that "twigs or staves were marked with certain
signs." We have found no characters more ancient
than Oghams and Ogham-Runes in Northern Europe,
and the conclusion is obvious.

I do not propose any attempt at determining
whether the Ogham was or was not " a steganography,
a cypher, a series of symbols ;" in fact, a secret form of
the Roman alphabet "used only by the initiated
among the pre-Christian and the Christian Gaoid-
heilg."[17] Dr. Graves has laboured hard to place the
abecedarium, not the characters,[18] in the rank of a
comparatively modern cryptogram, known to knights
and *literati*, and used chiefly for monumental and
magical purposes. He has proved conclusively that
the average of Ogham inscriptions are as simple as the
Etruscan, often consisting of a single proper name,
generally a genitive governed by " Lia " (*lapis
sepulchralis*), expressed or understood. In Ireland
it is accompanied by a patronymic ; in Etruria by a
matronymic ; the letters occur mixed with Runes,
and even with Latin, as Miss Margaret Stokes has
shown in her admirable volume of " Inscriptions."[19]

[17] "Hermothena," vol. iv., p. 400, and vol. v., pp. 208–252.

[18] The attention of the reader is called to the distinction between the
alphabetic order and the characters which compose the alphabet.

[19] Part IV., Plates ii. and iii. of "Christian Inscriptions in the Irish
Language," chiefly collected and drawn by George Petrie, LL.D., and

The Bishop of Limerick's elaborate and extensive arguments concerning the modern origin and the secret nature of Ogham appear to have been generally adopted.   Mr. Gilbert Gordie[20] expresses the popular opinion, "Oghams are, as we know, an occult form of monumental writing practised by the Celtic ecclesiastics of the early middle ages." The Maes Howe inscription appears to be a cryptogram, and the same is the case with its equivalent, the Arabic Mushajjar, or "Tree-Alphabet."

Professor Rhys[21] is the objector in chief to the Bishop of Limerick's theories and opinions. He holds that the "stepped" or "ladder" Ogham is purely artificial, and found chiefly in the "Essay on Ogham." He believes that the cryptic runes, from which the "fair writing" has been derived, are not proved old enough in any shape to originate the Ogham. He does not see any cause for accepting the assertion that "the Ogham alphabet was intended for cryptic purposes;[22] owning the while, "it is possible, however, that it may have, in the hands of pedants, been so applied, just as it was growing obsolete. He quotes (p. 302) from a well known member of the Royal Irish Academy, "Ogham inscriptions are of the simplest."

edited by Miss Stokes.   Also Cav. Nigra, *Reliquie Celtiche*, Turin, 1872. The oldest Roman alphabet found in Ireland is of the fifth century (O'Donovan, xxxvii).

[20] Vol. xii., part 1.   Edinburgh, 1877.   Proceedings of the Royal Society of Antiquaries, Scotland.

[21] "On Irish Ogham Inscriptions." A letter addressed (at special request) by John Rhys, M.A., late Fellow of Merton College, Oxford, to William Stokes, M.D., F.R.S., &c., President of the Royal Irish Academy, dated Rhyl, Oct. 28, 1874. Read Jan. 11, 1875.

[22] *Loc. cit.*, p. 301.

Professor Rhys,[23] treating of the Welsh inscriptions which date from the second century, shows
how the Ogmic alphabet, claimed for their own
country by certain Irish antiquaries, passed from
Wales to Ireland; and that the art, if ever invented by the Kelts, must have been due to the
ancestors of the Welsh. He believes, moreover,
that the Ogham, supposed to typify the rays of
light and similar poetic fancies, the rude system
used before the introduction of Runes, was borrowed
by the Kimri from their Teutonic neighbours. He
hazards a conjecture that though the origin is still
hidden in darkness, it was based upon the Phœnician—a conclusion apparently formed before reading
my letter to the *Athenæum*.[24] In his address to
that great scholar, the late William Stokes, he
would assign the chief part of the earlier class of
Irish Oghams to the sixth century, or, rather, to
the interval between the fifth and the seventh. He
suspects that one instance, at least, dates before the
departure of the Romans from Britain—especially
alluding to the Loghor altar examined by Dr. S.
Ferguson. He ends with saying, " It is noteworthy
that British Ogham-writing is to be traced back to a
time when we may reasonably suppose Kimric nation-
ality to have revived, and a reaction against Roman
habits and customs to have, to a certain extent,
taken place, when the last Roman soldier had taken

---

[23] " Lectures on Welsh Philology." London: Trübner, 1877. I know
the book only from Mr. O. H. Sayce's review (*The Academy*, May 12,
1877). It is out of print ; and we can only hope that the learned author
will listen to the voice of the publishers, who are clamouring for a
second edition.

[24] April 7, 1877.

his departure from our island.   But since the
Roman alphabet had been introduced into Britain,
it is highly improbable that another and a clumsier
one should have been invented and got into use.
The inevitable inference then seems to be, that
Ogmic-writing dates from a time anterior to the
introduction of the Roman alphabet."

Upon this part of the subject, Dr. now Sir
Samuel Ferguson, poet and scholar, informed me
that in one of the county histories of Cumberland,
whose author's name he had forgotten, a Palm-rune
attracted his attention.   He spent a long day at the
Shap Quarry, near Dalston, worked to supply the
Prætentura, or Southern Roman Wall of Hadrian or
Surrus, connecting the Tyne with the Solway Firth.
This interesting relic of an alphabet, which may
have dated from the days of the Latin Legionaries,
had unfortunately disappeared.   The " Cave-pit," at
Cissbury, near Worthing, shows at least one character,[25] and two imperfect cuts contain two Phœnician
and Etruscan *as* (Plate XXV, Figs. 1 and 2).   See
also " Inscribed Bone Implements," by J. Park
Harrison, M.A. : he divides the marks upon chalk
into two orders : Symbols and Simple signs.   Many of
the latter are Branch-Runes—*e.g.*, ᚠ ᚩ ᛏ ᛂᛟ and ᚦ

The most important evidence adduced by Prof.
Rhys in favour of his Teutonic-Kimric theory is, that
the third alphabetic letter the Jim (soft *g* as *G*eorge)
of the Arabs and Phœnicians ; and the Gimel (or hard
g as *G*orge) of the Hebrews and Greeks who pro-
nounce their Gamma as *Gh*amma, becomes a *ch*
(*Church*).   This fact, he says, can be explained only

[25] *Journal of the Anthropological Institute*, May, 1877, page 441.

on the supposition that the syllabary reached the Kelts through the Teutons.

According to the Uraicept, the "Bethluisnion" was invented by the Scythian King, Fenius Fear-saidh, who, about one generation before the Hebrew Exodus[26] came from his northern home and esta-blished a philological school of seventy-two students in the Plains of Shinar.[27]   In the "Book of Lecan" is found a tradition supposed to be interpolated, that, "Ogma, the sun-faced," brother of Breas, King of Ireland, both sons of Eladan or Elathan (*Sapientia*), in the days of the Teutonic (?) Tuath De Danaan, about nineteen centuries B.C., "invented the letters of the Scots, and the names belonging to them." Prof. Rhys opines that this mythical Irish hero was to be identified in ancient Gaul under the name "Ogmius," with the Roman Hercules, in the Welsh "Ofydd," a savant, the *Ovate* of the Eisteddfod. Kimric legend also traced the origin of letters to Ogyrven, father of the Dawn-goddess "Gwenh-wyfar" (Guinevere), the fabled wife of Arthur. Our author also opines that "Ogyrven" is, letter for letter, the Zend Angro-Maniyus or Ahriman, the bad-god of night and darkness and cold.   Here, then, we are in full Persia and amongst her sons, the Manichæans, of all sects perhaps the most vital and persistent.   But granting the Teutonic origin of Ogham, the question arises, says my erudite friend, Prof. Sprenger, "When and how did the Teutons borrow it from the Phœnicians ? "

---

[26] "Hermothena," vol. iv., pp. 452–53. The legend is universal in the ancient literature of Ireland.

[27] The date is given with considerable variations.

This much has been quoted from others. The first part of this paper may fitly end with my own work in the Orkney Islands ; it was the application of an Arabic alphabet to an Icelandic *graffito* in Palm-runes, Tree-runes, or Twig-runes, which the Bishop of Limerick would make the primitive form of Ogham. It is not a little curious that the mob of gentlemen who criticize with ease, has not, in a single case at least which came under my notice, remarked the curious discovery of a Scandinavian inscription in an Arabic character.

A ride to Hums, the classical Emesa, on February 27, 1871, and a visit to my old friend the Matrán or Metropolitan of the Nestorians, Butrus (Peter) introduced me to the alphabet known as El-Mus-hajjar, the tree or branched letters, one of the many cyphers invented by the restless Oriental brain. Shortly afterwards (June, 1872), I found myself inspecting Maes Howe, the unique barrow near Kirkwall (Orkneys), under the guidance of the late Mr. George Petrie, a local antiquary, whose energetic labours and whose courtesy to inquirers will long keep his name green.[28] The first sight of the Branch or Palm-Runes amongst the common Runes of Maes Howe reminded me of the alphabet which I had copied in northern Syria.

Mr. James Farrer, M.P. ("Notice of Runic Inscriptions discovered during Recent Excavations in the Orkneys," printed for private circulation, 1862), first "established the important fact of Runic inscriptions existing in Orkney, where none had hitherto been found." He gives (Plates VIII

[28] See " Ultima Thule," vol. i., pp. 285–87.

and IX) both sets of Palm-Runes, which run as follows :—

No. I.

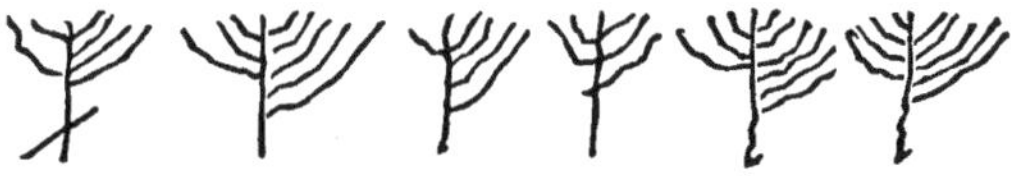

a (æ) *r* y i k r

Here the first "tree" has a cross-bar which Mr. Petrie acutely determined to represent the key of the cypher. This would be the first letter *á*, or, as in common Runic, the cognate diphthong (A E). He was thus able to read "Aeryikr" (Eric). Prof. Stephens, in his well-known work on the Tree or Twig-Runes, had interpreted the word AErling. But there is no *l* (), and the error may have arisen from the second letter having the lowest branch on the right *r*, cut short at the base (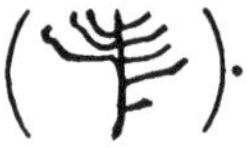).

No. II.

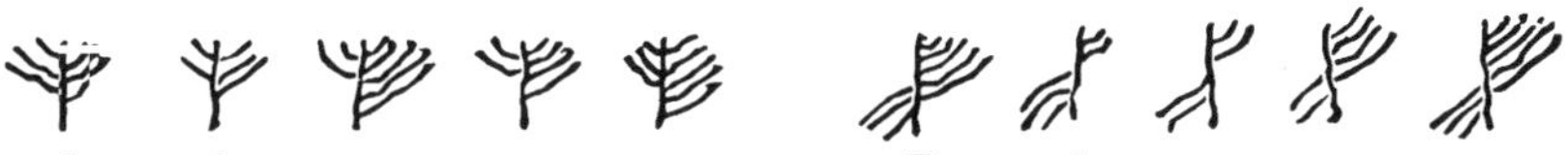

Th i s a *r* R ú n a r

The above, in which the left hand branches are bent downwards instead of upwards, proved equally amenable to its Œdipus. Prof. Stephens had also made it to mean "these Runes."

Thus Mr. Petrie had simply applied my Arabic "Mushajjar" to the Icelandic "Futhorc," or Scandinavian alphabet, so called, like the Abjad, the Bethluis and our own, from the letters which begin it.

No. III.

1 (Class) 2 (Class) 3 (Class)

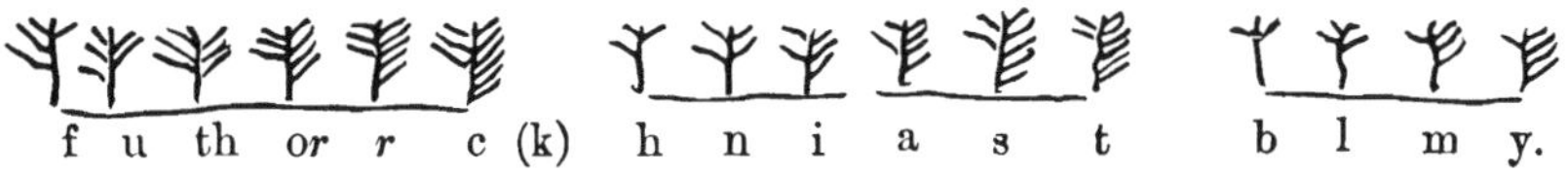

f u th *or* *r* c (k) h n i a s t b l m y.

Mr. Petrie announced his discovery as follows :—
"I attempted, by means of your 'tree-branched' alphabet to read the palm-runes of Maes Howe, but failed. It then occurred to me that they might correspond with the Futhorc, and, obtaining the key of the cypher, I completely succeeded after a few hours trial. On referring to Mr. Farrer's copies of the translation given by the Scandinavian professors, I find that Professor Stephens appears to have put five runes into the first two classes (?), which makes the third palm-rune (No. 1) to be *l*, instead of *y;* moreover, he does not give the key. My first attempt at classifying the Runes by means of the cypher, turned out correct ; and I have therefore retained that classification in reading the second inscription. It is evident that the classification could be altered at will of the person using it, and this uncertainty of arrangement must constitute the difficulty of interpreting such runes."

Mr. Farrer (Plates VIII and IX) gives both sets of Palm-runes, and borrows (p. 29, referring to Plate VIII) the following information from Professor Stephens :—" The six crypt-runes or secret staves represent the letters A, Æ, R, L, I, K, R, and signify Aalikr or Erling, a proper name, or perhaps the beginning of some sentence." Prof. Munch observes : " The other characters in the third line are known as ' Limouna,'[29] or Bough-Runes. They were used during the later times of the Runic period, in the same manner as the Irish Ogham, but are not here intelligible. The writer probably intended to represent the chief vowels, A, E, I, O, U, Y. The

---

[29] Generally " Lim-rúnar."

Runic alphabet was divided into two classes; the strokes on the left of the vertical line indicating the class, and those on the right the rune itself." And Professor Kunz declares, "The palm-runes underneath cannot be read in the usual manner; the first, third, and fourth of the runes being *a, o,* and *i*; the writer probably intended to give all the vowels, and some of the letters have been obviously miscarried, and have perhaps been altered or defaced at a later period by other persons. In the first of these, a cross-line has been added to show that the letter *a* is intended." Of No. XVIII (Plate X) Mr. Farrer notes : "The palm-runes are rarely capable of being deciphered. Prof. Munch similarly declares : " The bough-runes are not easy to decipher," whilst Cleasby (*sub voce*) explains them as "a kind of magical runes." They are mentioned in the Elder Edda (Sigrdrífurmál, Stanza II) :—

> " Line-runes thou must ken
> An thou a leach wouldst be
> And trowe to heal hurts."

A scholar so competent as Sir George Dasent assures me that he knows no other allusion to them in old Scandinavian literature.

The Bishop of Limerick believes that in this case "the Rune-graver has introduced his own name, evidently intending thereby to give a proof of his Runic accomplishments by the use of a cipher."[30] But Dr. Graves is possessed by the " dominant idea " of a cryptogram. In Nos. XIX and XX Plate X) we read, " Iorsafarar brutu Orkhröugh "

---

[30] " Hermothena," vol. iv., p. 463.

—the Jerusalem farers (pilgrims to the Holy Land) broke open Orkhow, the "shelter-mound." There are also seven crosses, and one inscription (No. XIII) must be read, Arab fashion, from right to left. We may therefore believe that certain old *Coquillards*, and possibly Crusaders, returning home with enlarged ideas, violated the tomb in search of treasure, an object especially Oriental; and put a single name and an unfinished inscription to warn followers that they had left nothing of value unplundered.

I cannot but hold this interpretation of a Scandinavian text by an Arabic character as proof positive that the Semitic "Mushajjar" and the Palm-runes of the Ogham and Runic alphabet are absolutely identical.

To conclude the subject of Ogham, with a notice of its derivation from the cuneiform of Babylon and Assyria and from the Phœnician. The former supposition has been much debated and even advocated, but not by Orientalists. Bishop Graves remarks[31] that although the arrow-headed characters include some phonetic signs, they rest mostly upon an idiographic base. His objection is not valid. The cuneiform alphabets, as everyone knows, gave rise, at an age anterior to Phœnician, to the Cypriot and pre-Cadmean syllabarium, used at Troy.[32] And finding a modified form of El-Mushajjar, in Pehlevi, one is tempted to refer it to the Persians, a restless and ingenious people who would have been more likely

[31] "Hermothena," vol. iv., pp. 471-72.
[32] See Schliemann's "Troy." Of the 18 inscriptions found in that valuable volume, 11 belong to the "Trojan stratum," and of these five are Cyprian.

than any Arabs to have converted its arrow-heads
into a cryptogram. The main objections to the
Phœnician theory are three : 1, the Phœnicians were
of Semitic stock, a race which borrows and improves
but does not originate : it is, in fact, remarkably
barren of invention ; 2, the Phœnicians, although
they used, as we know, letters in B.C. 500,[33] were
by no means a literary race. They doubtless corre-
sponded, engrossed, and kept their invoices and
their ledgers with exemplary care ; but with the
sole exception of the Ashmunazar or Sidonian
epitaph, that touching and beautiful wail over a
lost life, they have not left a single monument of
remarkable poetry or prose ; 3rd, and lastly, they
had a far handier alphabet of 22 letters chosen from
the Egyptian phonology, the latter being contained
in 25 characters besides some 400 hieroglyphics :
consequently they would hardly want a second.
Perhaps our Ogham may be of a still nobler stock,
and I here venture to suggest that it may have
originated with the far-famed Nabat or Nabathæans.

Finally, we may expect, when the subject shall
have acquired importance, to find traces of this
alphabet in places hitherto unsuspected. It may be
worth while to investigate the subject of the Runes[34]
found upon stones in the Vernacular lands. Some
scholars have interpreted them by the vernacular

---

[33] There is no known Phœnician inscription antedating B.C. 500
(M. Ernest Rénan, p. 138 of Schliemann's " Troy ") except only the
" Moabite Stone," if that noble monument be held Phœnician.

[34] Archiv für Sclavische Philologie. Berlin, 1877, 2 Band, 2ter Heft).
Mr. Howorth also refers me to vol. i., series 6, of the " Memoirs of
the Academy of St. Petersburgh."

tongues; whilst others look upon them as wholly
Scandinavian.   Mr. W. R. Morfill, of Oxford, a
competent scholar, believes the Glagolitic alphabet,
in which the supposed Slavonic Runes are stated to
be traced, to be of late introduction : others hold it
to be distinctly founded on Greek.

PART II.

El-Mushajjar. المشجر

In this part I propose to collect all the scattered
notices concerning the little-known Mushajjar, the
Arabic Tree-alphabet, adding the results of my own
observations.   Its birth is at present veiled in
mystery. I have heard of, but never have seen, rocks
and stones bearing the characters, and the manuscripts are by no means satisfactory.

In the spring of 1877, during my visit to Cairo,
that literary city of the Arabs appeared to be the
best place for investigating the origin of the
mysterious "Mushajjar."   Amongst those consulted
was the Aulic Councillor, Alfred von Kremer, the
ripe Arabic scholar of the *Culturgeschichte*, &c. : he
vainly turned over all the pages of the *Fihrist*,
(Flügel, Leipzig, 1871).   Prof. Spitta, Director of the
useful *Bibliotèque Khédiviale de l'Instruction publique*,

in the Darb El-Jemámíz, was not more fortunate.
Dánish Bey, Professor of Turkish to H.H. Ibrahim
Pasha, the young Prince now studying in England,
had heard of the cryptogram : he declared that it
should be called " El-Shajari" (the tree-shaped),
and thought that it was an Arab, not a Persian
invention. Fortunately I also consulted H.E. Yacoub
Artin Bey, an Armenian and Christian[35] officer, then
attached to the household of the same Prince ; and
the following is the result of our joint enquiries.

Moslem *literati* are, as a rule, painfully ignorant
of the history of language ; and, although many know
the words " El-Mushajjar " and " El-Shajari, " few
have any definite ideas upon the subject. I have
often heard reports of a manuscript which contains
a complete description of the character, but none
could tell us either the name of the book or of its
author. A popular tradition traces the origin of
the Arab Tree-runes to El-Húd,[36] the well-known
Himyarite prophet, buried in Hazramaut (Hazar-
maveth). Christian writers often identify him with
Heber, a hypothesis which Ibn Khaldún Tabari
disdainfully rejects. It is also reported that the

---

[35] "Tancred " declares that my friend's father, Artin Bey, was of
Israelitic blood. The name, in India Aratoon, is the Turkish form of
Haroutioune, meaning in Armenian "Resurrection." Imagine a
Hebrew choosing such cognomen ! The confusion arose from the
similarity of the Armenian Artin and the Hebrew Artom.

[36] The Koran (Sab, chap. vii., v. 66) sends him on a mission to the
Tribe of 'Ad, the Pelasgi of the Semites. He is supposed to have
lived about B.C. 1750, under the 'Adite King, Khul Khulján. The
Kámús gives his lineage as Bin 'Amir, b. Shálih b. Fálagh (Peleg?) :
b. Arphakhshad : b. Sám (Shem) : b. Núh·Sale (*loc. cit.*) and popular
opinion add two generations to these six. Húd b. 'Abdillah : b. Ribáh :
b. Kholúd : b. 'Ad : b. Aus (Uz) : b. Aram : b. Sám : b. Nuh.

alphabet was used in the reign of El-Maamún (XXVIth Abbaside Khalífah, A.D. 813 = 833). Yacoub Artin Bey had promised to procure for me, if possible, the volume containing this important notice.[37] Again, we trace it to the days of Abú 'l-Hazan Ali (Sayf el-Daulah), the literary Prince of Aleppo and Damascus (acc. A.H. 320 = A.D. 932 : ob. A.H. 356 = A.D. 966), when it was used for chronograms. Meanwhile that celebrated dictionary " El-Kámús " (of Ferozabádi A.D. 1350— 1414) declares that El-Mushajjar is a form of *Khat* (writing), and straightway passes on to another subject.

All we know for certain is that El-Mushajjar appears in two forms among the 80 alphabets recorded by Ibn Wahshiyah (Ahmad bin Abibakr). This author is called by Kirscher " Aben Vaschia " and " Vahschia," and by d'Herbelot (*sub voce* Faláhat), "Vahaschiah."[38] He is mentioned in the Kashf el-Zunún (Revelation of Opinions, &c.), by Haji Khalífah (ob. A. H. 1068 = A.D. 1658), as being employed in translating from Nabathæan into Arabic. Two other authorities quoted by Hammer[39] confirm the report. It is generally believed that he flourished in our ninth century ; that he finished his book about ·A.H. 214 (= A.D. 829),

---

[37] Unfortunately, the owner, who speaks highly of it, is a confirmed vagrant, in the habit of disappearing for months, and showing all the wild enthusiasm of his forefathers. He occasionally visits Cairo, in the vain attempt to make money out of a small estate. During 1877–78, the " Low Nile " so vexed him that he would neither lend the work or give its name.

[38] De Herbelot, however, calls him " Aboubekr ben Ahmed."

[39] Sect. xvi, " Ancient Alphabets," by Joseph Hammer. London : Bulmer, 1806.

or 1,040 years ago ; and in that year, as he himself
tells us, deposited the manuscript in the public
treasury founded by Abd el-Malik bin Marwán,
tenth caliph, A.D. 685—705 = A.H. 65—86.

Ibn Wahshiyah is a well known name, which has
given rise to abundant discussion, and of the latter
we have by no means seen the last.[40] I therefore
regret to see so trenchant an opinion expressed by Dr.
Charles Graves :[41] " an Arabic collection of alphabets
by Ibn Wahsheh,[42] translated by Hammer, contains
two tree-shaped alphabets, of which one is constructed on precisely the same principle as the
Ogham. This work, which for a time imposed upon
the half-learned, is now (1830) proved to be of no
authority." In his later publication the Bishop of
Limerick thus reforms his crude opinions—thirty-
six years have done their duty. " But the work,
apocryphal as it is, was written in the ninth or
tenth century ; and it will be a curious problem to
account for the similarity of the tree-alphabets
represented in it, and the ' Twig-Runes ' of
Scandinavia." This similarity it is my object to
illustrate, in the hope of restoring the Ogham to its
old home—the East. The work can be done only
by three means : 1, by proving that it was known
to the Moslems before the days of Ibn Wahshiyah ;
2, by showing that its wide diffusion and varied
forms suggest a more ancient origin ; and, 3, by
determining where it arose.

[40] I have outlined the subject in " The Gold Mines of Midian,"
chap. viii.
[41] Proceedings of Royal Irish Academy, vol. iv., p. 362, of 1830, de-
liberately repeated in " Hermothena," vol. iv., p. 465, of 1866.
[42] This error is Hammer's (*loc. cit.*).

The following are the varieties which I have hitherto been able to procure :—

No. I. (*Ibn Wahshiyah*).

حطى   هوز   ابجد

'i	t	h	.	z	w	h	.	d	j	b	a
10	9	8		7	6	5		4	3	2	1

تخذ   شت   قـر   سعفص   كلمن

z	kh	th	.	t	sh	v	k	.	s	f	a'	s	.	n	m	l	k
70	60	50		40	30	20			19	18	17	16	15		14	13	12	11

ضظغ

gh	z	z
100	90	80

No. II. (*Ditto*).

with the additionals—

No. III. (*A Modification of the above*).

with the addition of a distinct character for ل

= lú)

No. IV. (from Hums).

No. V. (from ditto).

No. VI.

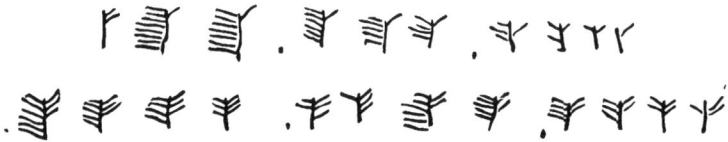

It is to be noticed that all these modifications are read from right to left, and are disposed in the Hebrew order ; this, which differs. from the common form mostly by placing the additional Arabic letters at the end, is still known as El-Abjad, after its four initial characters. The Moslems trace this dis-position backwards through the Prophet Húd to Father Adam ; but we hold that it was adopted about the beginning of the Christian era when the Himyaritic characters became obsolete. The terms El-Mushajjar and El-Shajari (the branched or the tree-shaped) are evidently Arabic. But, as shown by the Icelandic "Limb-runes," the syllabary may have had various vernacular names invented by every race that adopted it. This artless article is evidently capable of universal application. It may be written from left to right, as well as *vice versâ*, and it is equally fitted for expressing English and Arabic. Like the Ogham, it is slow and cumbrous ; but so are all alphabets in which the letters are detached. The Fleasgh or directing-line which appears in No. IV and in the Ogham, is general to the Hindú alphabets, whose source was the Phœnician. The latter, probably in a pre-Cadmean form, passed eastwards from Syria as a centre, *viâ* Southern or Himyaritic Arabia, to the vast Indian Peninsula, which was apparently unalphabetic before B.C. 350. Thence, altered once more, it was spread by the Buddhists through Central Asia as far as the Wall of China. Westward, the Greeks, the Etruscans and the Romans carried it over the length and breadth of Europe; and our daily A, B, C, D still represents the venerable Hebrew-Arabic Abjad and the Greek Alpha, Veta, Ghamma, Thelta.

The following are Ibn Wahshiyah's remarks upon the six forms given above :—

No. 1 is "The alphabet of Dioscorides the Doctor (Dískoridús el-Hakím), commonly called El-Mushajjar. He wrote on trees, shrubs and herbs, and of their secret, useful and noxious qualities in this alphabet, used since in their books by different philosophers."[43]

No. 2 is "The alphabet of Plato, the Greek Philosopher. It is said that each letter of this alphabet had different imports, according to the affair and the thing treated of."[44]

No. 3, which evidently modifies No. 2, was copied for me by my friend Yacoub Artin Bey. In the library of the late Mustafá Pasha (Cairo) he found an undated manuscript (ρ No. i), apparently not ancient : upon the margin of the last page, probably for want of a better place, had been copied the "Khatt Shajari." It is the full Arabic, as compared with the incomplete

---

[43] Ibn Wahshiyah, in Hammer ; Sect. xvi., pp. 8 and 38.
[44] *Ibid.*, pp. 9–46.

Hebrew alphabet ; with a terminal addition of " Lá."
The latter both in the Abjad and in the popular
system is written otherwise than might be expected.

No. 4 is the only system that has a base line, and
its elements appear in the fourteen letters which
conclude No. 2 ; it is one of those which I copied at
Hums, and it contains only the ancient and universal
Semitic letters, lacking the last six of Arabic.

No. 5, also copied at ·Hums, is based upon the
same system as the former ; but the scribe gave
warning that it is applied to Pehlevi or old Persian,
whereas No. 4 is Arabic.

No. 6 is found in a manuscript called *El-Durar el-
Muntakhabát fi Isláh el-Ghalatát el-Mashhúri*, or
" Pearls Choice and Scattered, in Rectification of
vulgar Errors." It was translated from Arabic into
Turkish in A.H. 1221 (= A.D. 1805) ˙and its
information is distinctly borrowed from Ibn Wahshiyah's *Shauk El-mushtahá fi Ma'rifat Rumúz el-
Aklám* (" Desirable Advice in the knowledge of the
Secrets of written Characters "). As regards the
assertion that Dioscorides wrote in the *Kalám el-
Mushajjar* (Tree-shaped characters), perhaps the
Arabic version of the Greek physician was made in
this cryptogram ; and the work of the translator or
the scribe was eventually attributed by confusion to
the author.

PART III.

Various Notes on Ogham-Runes and El-Mushajjar.

A correspondent in the United States, who does
not wish to be named, draws my attention to the
Lycian characters on the Xanthus Tomb and other
casts and monuments in the British Museum.[45]
During the last generation. some thirty years ago, it
was the general opinion that the language of these
epigraphs had some connection with Zend, and the
characters with Greek.   A few of the letters
resemble Ogham-runes and El-Mushajjar : for instance, the characters below the alphabets (*loc. cit.*)
are true runes ꟿ ⸳ ⱱ⸳ and ꞃ   Mr. Sharpe suggests
that they are imperfect copies of ⱱ⸴ E or F.   The
other letters are apparently Phœnicio-Greek.   I am
also told that a similar family likeness appears in
the coins called by Sestini[46] " Celtiberian;" and which
M. Grassin,[47] with the generality of numismatologists,
sets down as *médailles inconnues.*

Another correspondent threw out the following
hint regarding " The Coins of the Eastern Khalifáhs

[45] See " An Account of Discoveries in Lycia," by Sir Charles Fellows.
London : Murray, 1840.   Especially the Lycian letters in p. 442, and
Appendix B, "On the Lycian Inscriptions," by Daniel Sharpe.   Also
vol. i., pp. 193–196, Proc. of the Philological Society, Feb. 23, 1844.
[46] " Classes générales," 4to.   Florentiæ, 1841.
[47] " De l'Ibérie, 8vo.   Leleux : Paris, 1838.

of the British Museum," by S. Lane Poole (vol. i,
p. 175). *Croyez-vous que les arbrisseaux, au revers
des médailles Sassanides, aient quelque rapport avec
cette écriture?* He adds, "I find in the above volume
'Copper Coinage, Amawee, with formula of faith
only.'"

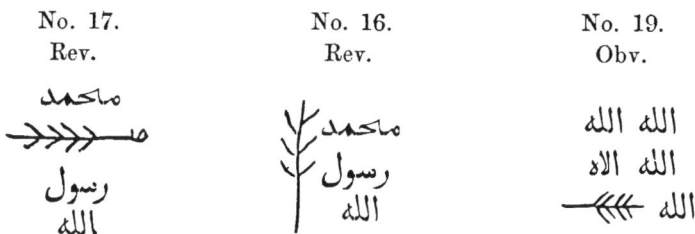

No. 17. Rev.	No. 16. Rev.	No. 19. Obv.
محمد رسول الله	محمد رسول الله	الله الله الله الاه الله

"The subjoined contains the name of the mint
(Tiberias) and bears no date :—

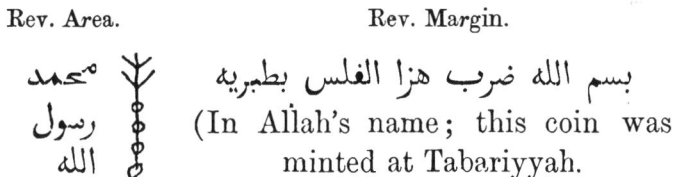

Rev. Area.	Rev. Margin.
محمد رسول الله	بسم الله ضرب هزا الفلس بطبريه (In Allah's name; this coin was minted at Tabariyyah.

"Now the earliest copper coins in the British
Museum bear the date A.H. 92, and these evidently
precede it, so that we may refer them to A.H. 77."

On the other hand I would remark that, in the
four specimens given above, the "twigs" appear to
be merely ornamental, being always in two; three,
or four pairs, hence we must prefer the opinion of
Prof. Stickel of Jena (*Muhammedanische Munz-
kunde*), followed by Mr. Bergmann of the Museum,
Vienna, that they are either mint-signs, denoting
the places of issue, Tiberias, Hamah, and Damascus;
or that they are merely intended to fill up the area,
like the circlets, the elephants, and other animals
which appear upon the coins of Abd el-Malík bin

Merwán and various of the Ommiades. In those days the Moslems were not so squeamish about representing things of life and even the human form. For instance, Tiberias issued a coin bearing on the obverse a robed figure standing upright with sword and bandolier slung over the shoulder. On the reverse is a Byzantine vase with a globe instead of a cross. The inscription, in detached characters resembling those of the Nabat (Nabathæans) is *Khálid ibn Walíd, Zuríba fí Tabariyyah.* I may note that the Bayt el-Khalidí, the descendants of the Conqueror of Syria, still flourish at Jerusalem.

The Rev. Dr. Badger also pointed out to me. in the *Exposé de la Religion des Druzes,* by that celebrated Orientalist, Silvestre de Sacy,[48] the following figure of Mohammed borrowed from the pages of El-Nuwayri, and composed of $m+h+m+d$, beginning as usual from the right.

The French author adds : " *Pour y trouver l'allusion que l'on cherche, on écrit le mot perpendiculairement, et on altère un peu la forme des lettres, ou peut-être on leur conserve une forme plus ancienne.*" Some fifteen years ago Dr. Badger copied a true monogram from a copper plate found at Aden, expressing the words *Wa Sallam* (Adieu), *i.e.,* $w + s + l + m$.

Travelling to Alexandria in October, 1877, with Dr. Heinrich Brugsch-Bey, I showed him my letter

---

[48] Paris, Imprimerie Royale, 1838.   Introd. to vol. i., p. lxxxvi.

to the *Athenæum ;*[49] and that distinguished Egyptologist at once recognised several of the forms. In
1867-68, happening to be at Agram, he was in-
duced, little expecting that a new alphabet would
be the result, to unroll an unopened mummy belonging to the Museum. Its date appeared to be 700—
500 years, B.C. ; and he was not a little surprised to
find the swathes, some of them 20 feet long, covered
not with hieroglyphs, but 'with characters partly
Græco-European (?) and partly Runic ; at any rate
non-Egyptian. The writing was divided, by regular
lacunæ, into what appeared to be chapters, each
consisting of 10-12 lines, and the whole would
make about 60 octavo pages. We could not help
suspecting that he had found a translation of the
Todtenbuch from Egyptian into some Arabic (Nabathæan ?) tongue. This Nilotic Bible, whose title
Dr. Birch renders " The Departure from the Day "
(*i.e.,* death), is supposed to date from B.C. 3000, and
thus it would precede Moses by some fifteen centuries. It is divided into eighteen books, containing 150 to 165 chapters in various manuscripts. The
general conception is that the future is simply a
continuation of the present life ; and chapter 110,
treating of existence in Elysium, notices the com-
munications of spirit-friends.

The following is Dr. Brugsch's transcript of the
alphabet—21 characters—

ㄱＩ�٩A┼ﾉﾘRﾏﾆつﾣﾔ﹨ ∪⅄ ⅄ΚＨﾘﾔ⚡

I immediatcly wrote to my friend, the Abbé
Ljubié, Custos of the Museo del Triregno, Agram.

He replied (November 26th, 1877) that it would be difficult to copy the swathes as the marks were doubtful, and that a competent photographer, Herr. Standl, had failed to reproduce them in sun-picture. The colour of the cloth had been darkened by time to a dull yellow, and the letters refused to make an impression ; perhaps, however, a better instrument might have succeeded. The idea of washing the *fascie* (swathings) white was rejected for fear of obliterating the marks.

Two years before the date of my application the Oriental Society of Leipzig had addressed the Directors of the Museum, requesting a loan of the *bende* (bandages), but the Government had refused ; promising, however, to aid the studies of *savants* charged with the transcription. And here the matter had dropped. At the instance of Dr. Leo Reinisch, the well-known Professor of Egyptology to the University, Vienna, Abbé Ljubié proposed to reproduce in print these *pannilini* (little cloths) and other interesting remains under his charge ; but the " necessary " in the shape of a subsidy of public money was not forthcoming.

On June 4th, 1878, I received another letter from the Abbé, giving the history of the mummy as follows. According to the Museum registers, about half a century ago, one Michiele Burié, a *concepista* (inferior employé) of the Hungarian Aulic Chancellerie, brought it back with him from Egypt. The owner left it as a dying gift to his brother Elia, parish priest of Golubince, in Slavonía, and sub-deacon in the diocese of Dyakovar, where now resides the far-famed Mgr. Strossmeyer. This ecclesiastical owner also dying, the mummy found its way to the Museum, packed, as it still is, in two modern chests, the horizontal containing the bandages and inner parts, and the vertical, the skeleton nude and propped by an iron bar.   It is complete in all its parts ; the hair is thick and well-preserved ; and traces upon the brow suggest that the head had been partly gilt.   According to the Abbé Ljubié, Dr. Brugsch, who inspected the mummy after it had been unrolled by others, pronounced it to be *Cretan.*

Traces of writing are shown by seven fragments, whose measure in mètres is as follows :—

No. 1 = 0·358 long × 0·065 broad.
 „   2 = 0·182 „   × 0·060   „
 „   3 = 0·282 „   × 0·052   „
 „   4 = 0·260 „   × 0·050   „
 „   5 = 0·215 „   × 0·055   „
 „   6 = 0·146 „   × 0·062   „
 „   7 = 0·133 (?)   × 0·045   „

A local photographer, Sig. Pommer, at last succeeded in making a copy.   The latter was sent to Prof. Leo Reinisch, who concluded his reply with ; *" Vorläufig nur meine Ueberzeugung, dass wenn es Ihnen gelingt, die Inschriften zu publiciren, dieselben ein enormes Aufsehen in den gelehrten Kreisen machen werden."*   The Egyptologist was requested to apply for a subsidy to I. R. Academy of Sciences, Vienna, or to obtain subscriptions for covering the expenses of publication.   Nothing of the kind, however, seems to have been done.

During my absence in Midian, Mrs. Burton sent

to Agram, for the purpose of copying the inscription, Mr. Philip Proby Cautley, of Trieste, who at first was looked upon as a rival photographer. Sig. Pommer had aspired to making a "good job" : he asked ten florins for photographing each fourth of what may be looked upon as a chapter. On January 22nd, 1878, Mr. Cautley wrote to me as follows :—

"On the morning of my arrival at Agram I called on Abbé Ljubić, who received me most cordially, and put himself entirely at my disposal. I then inspected the bandages, of which many had been unswathed, and had been removed to the Director's study from the antiquarian department of the Museo del Triregno, where the mummy stands. Though well preserved on the whole, the greater part is illegible ; time and the exudations of the dead have stained them dark-brown. They consist of linen-strips, varying from one to three yards in length, and cut off the piece, as they show no selvage. The breadth is about two inches ; the stuff would be called coarse in our days, the warp and woof are equally thick ; and the texture of the linen is very even.

"The writing is divided into sections of five or six lines each, measuring about seven and a half inches long, according to the length of the cloth. These must have been in hundreds ; and one of the best specimens was shown to me at the town photographer's. Each piece appears to have been a chapter, separated by intervals of about two fingers breadth. The Abbé styled the characters *Græco antico mischiato con caratteri jeratichi;* and he thinks that the mummy dates from the third or fourth cen-

No. I.

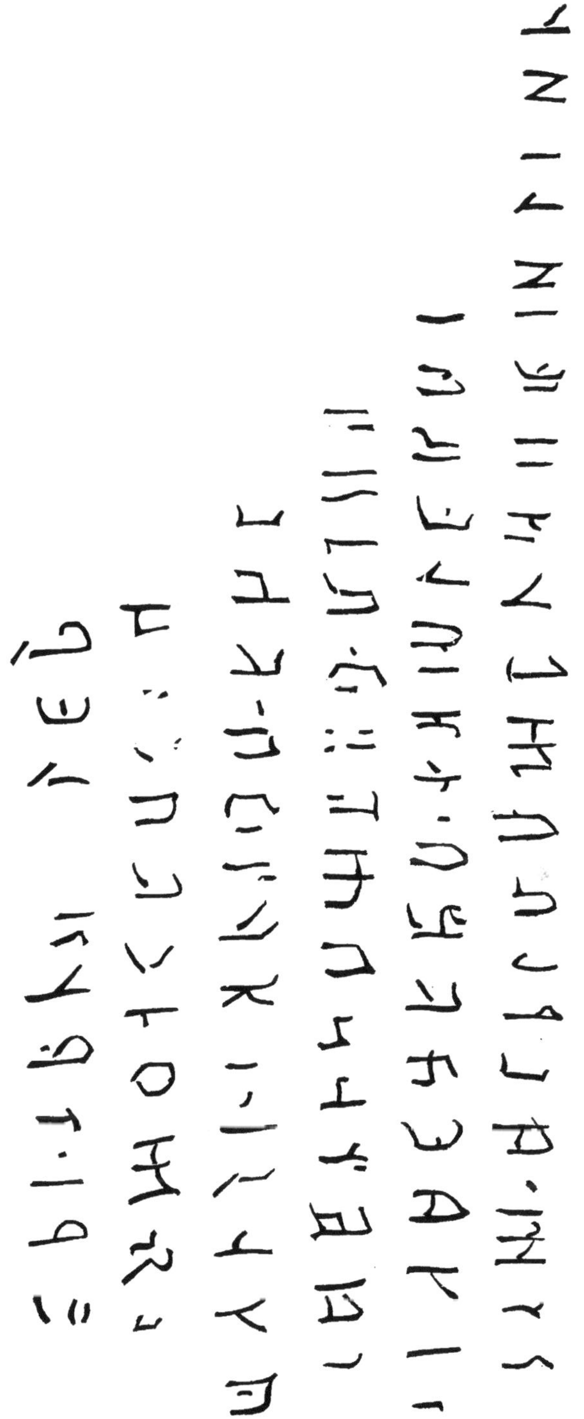

HARRISON & SONS, LITH. ST MARTINS LANE, W.C.

HARRISON & SONS, LITH. ST. MARTINS LANE, W.C.

Gap.

Two lines wanting.

HARRISON & SONS, LITH. S? MARTINS LANE, W.C.

tury. A.D.[50]   The Græco-hieratic idea may have
arisen from the condition of the thick strokes, which
extended originally over one and even two threads;
now they have been erased on the upper part of the
thread, so as to leave marks, often double, in the
intervening spaces only.   I mentioned to the Director my intention of copying the characters on
tracing-cloth; the simplicity of the idea seemed to
excite his merriment.   However, next morning he
admired the results obtained, and he asked me to
leave some of the material so that he might try his
hand.

" Choosing a well-marked chapter, I went to work
by pinning a piece of tracing-cloth over it, and then
following the characters as exactly as possible with a
pencil.   Curious to say, the tracing-cloth, instead of
preventing the characters being seen, or rendering
them more indistinct, brought them out, I suppose
by uniting the two strokes formed by the ink having
been erased on the single threads.   The work was
continued as long as I could find a piece clear enough
to be copied, and where the characters were near
enough to one another for deciphering.

" The copies have been numbered from 1 to 5.
In No. 3 you will remark that two lines are wanting
at the bottom.   The original does not show any
stains or marks that could have been characters,
while the three top lines are distinct.   I take it,
therefore, to have been the end of a chapter, or
perhaps of the whole volume.   No. 4 shows on the

[50] Dr. Brugsch-Bey, who upon these subjects is perhaps the highest
living authority, assigns, as has been seen, the mummy to the fifth
century B.C.

right hand a break in the manuscript which has
been denoted by a dotted line.".

So far Mr. Cautley, who did his work carefully and
completely. I give it *in extenso*.

The following appears to be the alphabet. The
signs number 27 ; but two of them are so similar to
others that they may be omitted, thus reducing the
total to 25 : the number assigned by Plutarch to the
hieroglyphic :—

Lastly, as regards the Agram mummy, I have
received a promise from my learned friend, Dr. H.
Brugsch-Bey, to send me his copies of the inscriptions
taken from what he calls this *trésor inconnu*.

We have now reached B.C. 500 ; but we may go
further back.[54] Dr. Schliemann's learned volume
("Troy and its Remains," London : Murray, 1875)
shows, among the *monuments figurés*, not a few
specimens of lines so disposed that, without having
Ogham or El-Mushajjar on the brain, I cannot but
hold them to be alphabetic. A few instances will
suffice. We find the following two forms Γ and Υ
on an inscribed terra-cotta seal (p. 24), which may
consequently be presumed to be significant ;[55] and
there is something very similar on the "Piece of

[52] App. Brugsch (||) reversed.

[53] The same.

[54] The Siege of Troy would be about B.C. 1200, and the foundation of
the city B.C. 1400. Thus 200 years would be allowed to the five Kings,
Dardanus, Ericthonius, Tros, Ilus, and Laomedon, preceding Priam.

[55] See seal No. 78, with signs resembling the ancient *Koppa* stamped
upon the coins of Corinth.

Red Slate, perhaps a whetstone" (*ibid.*).   In p. 130,
"Terra-cotta with Aryan emblems," the figure to
the right shows the following distinct types : 1, ⅍
(repeated with equal symmetry in whorl No. 376,
Pl. XXVII), 2, ⅙ 3, ⅍ (see also whorl No. 400, Pl.
XXXIII), and 4, ⅎ , No. 164, p. 235.   These can
hardly be modifications of "Aryan symbols," as
the unexplained *Rosa mystica*; the well-known
Swastika ⅏ the εὖ ἐστι, the signs of fire and of
good wishes, and the original cross, especially its
modification, the Maltese ; nor signs of lightning ;
nor mere branch ornaments, as on the "elegant
bright-red vase of terra-cotta" (p. 282) ; nor "sym-
bolical signs" as on the cylinder (p. 293).

Again, the "Terra-cotta Vase from the house of
Priam" (p. 308) gives the peculiar ⅍.   It may be
only an ornament, like the "Greek honeysuckle,"
the simplified form of the Assyrian "Hom" or Tree
of Life, the Hindu "Soma"; but the difference of
number in the branches on both sides of the perpendicular, suggests something more.   Many of the
whorls again show what may be "Palm-runes."   I
will quote only two.   No. 309 (Pl. XXI) bears
with six lines to the proper left and nine to the
right. On whorl 399 (Pl. XXXIII) we have a
variety of similar forms ⅍ ⅍ , ⅎ , or ⅍,

♓, or ♓, ♒, and ♑.   On whorl No.

494 (Pl. LI), are inscribed ♒ and ♒ ; whilst
whorl No. 115, the lines Nos. 145, 146 and No. 496
as determined by Prof. Gomperz, bear letters alphabetic and Cypriote.   Dr. Schliemann is confident
that these existed in Homeric Troy, although Homer
uses the word γράφειν in two places only with the
sense of " to grave " (scratch into).

It is not a little curious that Schliemann's other
great work (" Mycenæ," &c., London : Murray,
1878), with its 549 illustrations and 25 plates,
contains no sign which can be considered alphabetic,
and very few of the branch forms numerous at Troy.
I find only two instances : one of the Γ twice repeated in No. 48 (Pl. XI) ; and the other in No. 102
(Plate XVIII) where ʃ occurs with Ͻ thrice repeated.

The age of the items forming Dr. Schliemann's
great finds can be settled approximatively with
comparative ease.   This is not the case with Cyprus.
General L. P. di Cesnola (" Cyprus," &c., London :
Murray, 1877) believes that his terra-cottas mostly
date from B.C. 400–300 ; but evidently there are
articles which run up to the days of Sargon, B.C. 707.
Here, again, I find only two instances of what may
be " branched Runes."   One is on a pottery ʲjar
(Plate XLII, fig. 2), which shows the combination
of the human figure with the geometric pattern :
the proper left of the standing warrior bears without any similar sign on the corresponding field.
Again, in Plate XLI (Gem No. 22) occurs a double

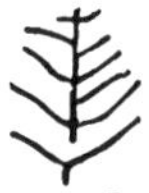 with five branches on the proper right, and six to the left; both are surrounded by an oval of beads or circlets. In p. 391, it is explained as a "sacred leaf (or tree)": perhaps the Persea plum whose resemblance to a tongue made it a symbol of the Deity amongst the ancient Egyptians. But here, again, there is an evident want of symmetry. Compare it with the regular forms of the tree branches (Plate XI, p. 114), which are probably flags growing below the papyri, on the silver patera found at Golgos or Golgoi, north of Larnaka. In Plate XXXVI (Gem No. 5), we have four letters 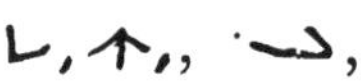, and , faced by the cone and circle supposed to represent the conjunction of Baal-Ammon with Ashtaroth.

It appears highly probable that Palm-runes and El-Mushajjar were known to the ancient Etruscans, possibly through Egypt.[56] Sir Samuel Ferguson kindly forwarded to me the following transcript of signs which occurred on a sepulchral urn of clay found in the Tirol, with other objects of decidedly Rasennic provenance: —

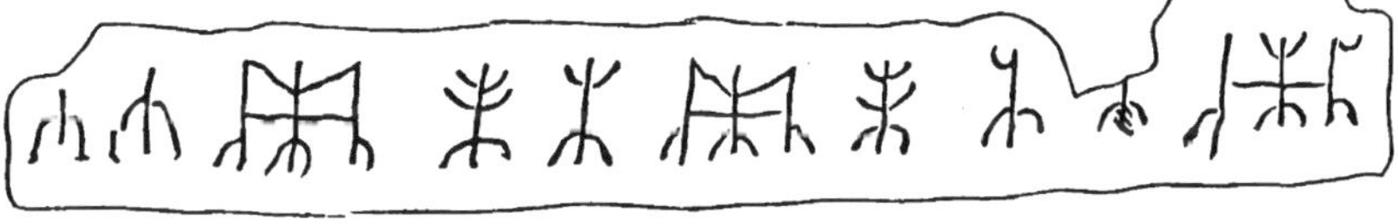

As will be observed, there are frequent repetitions as well as diversities in the signs; and my learned correspondent was of opinion that the latter were

[56] Upon the subject of the Etruscans in Egypt, see pp. 106–114 of the *Bulletin de l'Institut d'Égypte*, No. xiii., of 1875.

not sufficient to establish a distinctly alphabetic character.

Amongst the finds at the cemetery of Marzabotto, dating from at least 1000 B.C., I find the following Etruscan mark ·—[57]

Again, my attention was drawn to Etruria by the fine folio, *Intorno agli Scavi archeologichi*[58] (in the Arnealdi property), near Bologna, lately published by the Count Senator G. Gozzadini, whose long labours have done so much in illustrating the condition of early remains in his native land.

Page 32 offers a highly interesting talk of *Sigle* ("potters' marks") from various cemeteries, especially that of Villanova. The destruction of the latter settlement was determined by the Count, from the presence of an *æs rude*, to date about B.C. 700, or the Age of Numa. M. de Mortillet,[59] on the other hand, would make it much older.

The table in question is divided into four heads: 1, those scratched (*graffiti*) on the base of the articles after baking ; 2, the marks on other parts of the pottery also baked ; 3, the basal *graffiti* made after the oven had done its work ; and 4, the signs inscribed upon bronze vases. No. 1, numbering 39, supplies

[57] Table III., p. 2, " Marche figularie condotte a graffiti, nei vasi sco-perti nella Necropoli di Marzabotto." Primo Supplemento. Parte Prima. Roma, &c., 1872.

[58] Bologna ; Fava e Garagnani, 1877.

[59] Pp. 88–89 " Le Signe de la Croix avant le Christianisme," &c.

seven more or less connected in shape with the
Palm-runes, without including the crosses which
may belong to any age. The ┌ the ┤ and the
ᛦ are perfect with their variants, the ✕ ┤ and
the ⚹. Less remarkable are the ⋏ the ⇃ and
the seven-branched tree 🌿. No. 2 gives four
types : viz., the ⅂, the ⋏, the ⚹, and the ⌡ :
in this category the five crosses are noticeable, varying from the simple ┼ to a complex modification of
the Swastika (卐): that peculiarly Aryan symbol
which gave rise first to the Christian "Gammadion,"
and lastly to the Maltese Cross. No. 3 gives three
signs : the ⊥, the ┤, and the ⊢, besides the
two crosses plain (✕) and crotchetted (✕). Lastly,
No. 4 gives two : the ┤ and the ⅄. In Table 1,
also, we find the Phœnician Alif (⋉), and the
same occurs eight (nine ?) times in the *Sigle,* which
are printed (p. 236) in my little volume upon
" Etruscan Bologna."

I venture to suggest that these *graffiti* are true
letters and not mere marks.   Similarly in the
Wusúm ("tribal signs") of the Bedawin, we find
distinct survival, real significance underlying what
seems to be simply arbitrary.   For instance, the
circlet affected by the great 'Anezah, or Central
Arabian family, is the archaic form of the Arabic
Ayn, the Hebrew Oin, which begins the racial
name.

The following communication to the *Archæographo Triestino*[60] suggests a further extension of the system also possibly Etruscan.

In September, 1876, I had occasion to visit the island-town Ossero, in the Gulf of Fiume, whose waters bathe the southern and the south-eastern shores of the Istrian peninsula. Landing at La Cavanilla, an ancient Suez Canal in miniature, spanned by a bridge right worthy of the Argonautic days, we were met by his Reverence Don Giovanni Bolmarcich, Archiprete of the Community, who was good enough to show us his finds and the places which had produced them. Amongst the number was a common-shaped sepulchral lamp (*lume eterno*) which struck me forcibly. The inscribed lines may have been, as suggested by the learned Dr. Carl Kunz, Director of the Museum of Antiquities, Trieste, the trick of a waggish apprentice; but they are disposed upon a true Fleasgh or Runi-Staff, which mere scratches would hardly be, and there is evident method in their ordering. If it be asked what El-Mushajjar and Ogham-Runes have to do in the Archipelago of Istria, I reply that " Palm-runes " appear in impossible places; and that the Lion of Marathon, which named the Piræus *Porto Leone*, and which still stands before the Arsenal, Venice, is covered as to the shoulders with legible Runic inscriptions. The following illustration shows the lamp in natural size, and the marks were drawn for me, in order to correct and control my own copy, by Don Giovanni.

---

[60] Fascicolo ii., vol. v. of 1877.

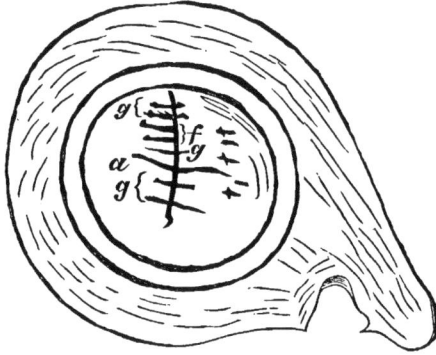

Amongst the impossible places where Ogham and Mushajjar-like lines appear must be included the tattoo of the New Guinea savages. Mr. Park Harrison has given the "characters tattooed on a Motu woman" from the south-eastern coast, whose arms, especially the right, and both whose breasts bare such types as ∧Υ and ∧. Philologists will bear in mind the curious resemblance which has been traced between Phœnician characters and the Rejang alphabet of Sumatra, which is mostly Phœnician inverted. In fact, it would not surprise me if future students established the fact that the whole world knows only one alphabet (properly so called), and that that is Phœnician.

I here conclude for the present my notices of the connection between the Ogham-Runes, "whose origin is still hidden in darkness," and the equally mysterious "Mushajjar," or Arabic-branched alphabet. Prof. J. Rhys, let me repeat, believes that the former is "derived in *some* way from the Phœnician alphabet"; but he holds his theory to be "highly hypothetical"; and he "would be only too glad to substitute facts for suppositions." It is my conviction that Ogham descends from an older and even nobler stock. I hope some day to restore it to the East, and to prove that, in the former *El-Mushajjar*, it originated among the Nabathæo-Chaldeans. It would, indeed, be curious if the Ogham alphabet of the old schoolmaster, King Fenius (the Phœnician ?), concerning whom Irish tradition speaks with such a confident and catholic voice, should once more be traced back to the Plains of Shinar.

RICHARD F. BURTON.

Harrison & Sons, Printers in Ordinary to Her Majesty, St. Martin's Lane.